RICKMANSWORTH
A Pictorial History

The armorial bearings of the Urban District Council of Rickmansworth, obtained on 2 June 1953.

RICKMANSWORTH
A Pictorial History

Adrienne and Christopher Jacques

on behalf of the
Rickmansworth Historical Society

Phillimore

1996

Published by
PHILLIMORE & CO. LTD.,
Shopwyke Manor Barn, Chichester, West Sussex

ISBN 1 86077 027 4

Printed and bound in Great Britain by
BIDDLES LTD.
Guildford, Surrey

Dedicated to the memory of
Godfrey Cornwall

List of Illustrations

Frontispiece: Armorial Bearings of the Urban District Council

Acknowledgements

The authors acknowledge permission from the following to reproduce their photographs: Aero Films of Borehamwood, 80, 101; authors' collection, 157; Birmingham Public Libraries for the Francis Frith Collection, front cover, 4, 7, 16, 24, 45, 67, 68, 120, 124, 154, 88, 128, 129, 136, 171, 173; Mr. S. Bodkin, 101; the family of F.L. Dickins, 34; Hertfordshire County Council Local Studies collection, 21, 78, 125, 131; Hertfordshire County Council Record Office, 74, 130; Rickmansworth Historical Society for the Godfrey Cornwall slide collection, 1-3, 5, 9, 10, 12-15, 17-18, 20, 22, 23, 26-29, 31, 35-37, 39-44, 46-48, 49-52, 54, 56-59, 62-66, 71-73, 75-77, 79, 81, 82, 86, 90-100, 102-105, 106-119, 121-123, 126, 132-135, 137-143, 145-147, 149-153, 155, 158, 159, 163-170, 174, back cover; Rickmansworth Library Local Collection, 6, 8, 11, 19, 25, 30, 32, 33, 55, 60, 61, 69, 70, 83-85, 127, 144, 148, 156, 160, 161; Mr. G. Saul, 87; Mr. R. Waldock, 53, 89, 162; *Watford Observer*, 38, 172. The copyright of photograph number 21 is held by Kevin S. Whelan whom we have endeavoured to trace to obtain permission to reproduce.

The authors wish to thank members of the Rickmansworth Historical Society who so readily offered photographs and postcards for inclusion in this pictorial history; and the many friends who provided information about the photographs.

In particular, they appreciate the encouragement and administrative help given in producing this book by Mr. G.M. Saul, the society's chairman, and for his final blessing on its contents.

They also wish to record their thanks to Marie Staunton and staff of Rickmansworth library without whose forbearance this book would not have been produced; and also to Marilyn and Anna of Vantage Chemists for their unceasing smiles when presented with yet another batch of black and white slides from which to make prints; and to Mrs. Susan Sharp of Fotocolour who arranged for the production of these prints.

Introduction

Rickmansworth, in the south-west corner of Hertfordshire, is situated in a river valley between the foothills of the Chilterns and the hill plateau of northern Middlesex. The town lies at the confluence of the river Colne with the rivers Chess and Gade, two streams which have their source in the chalk of the Chiltern Hills.

Before the last Ice Age the precursor of the river Thames flowed eastwards through this valley on its journey to the North Sea depositing beds of gravel in which can be found many flint scrapers and hand axes of prehistoric man. The last Ice Cap pushed down from the north east blocking the flow of the river which thereby formed a gigantic lake covering most of present-day south-west Hertfordshire. By the time the ice retreated, the river Thames had cut a more southerly route leaving its former valley to become the bed of the river Colne which flowed westward to join the river Thames at Staines.

The area surrounding the confluence of the three rivers was left as a marshy swamp bordered by fertile upper reaches where the waters of the former lake had subsided. This land was soon covered in dense vegetation and Stone-Age man found the valley a valuable source of animal and plant life. Archaeological evidence has shown the existence of a prehistoric causewayed settlement at Hampermill, a mile or so north of the confluence where the river Colne could be crossed in comparative safety. Two substantial finds of Bronze-Age implements have also been discovered in the Rickmansworth area but there is little evidence of permanent settlement until the time of the Belgic Catuvellauni people. This tribe were conquered by Julius Caesar and the Roman Army in 55 B.C. but negotiated a treaty of trade and protection with their Roman oppressors.

A hundred years later the Romans settled in Britain, and rebuilt Verlamio, the head-quarters of the Catuvellauni, as a regional headquarters in their expanding empire. Roman Verulamium, situated on Watling Street, became the third most important city in the province of Britain, containing impressive public buildings including an amphitheatre. The city was the focus of a wide hinterland whose farming activities sustained the city dwellers and provided country estates for their wealthier citizens.

Some trackways through the local woodland were upgraded to the standard of Roman roadways, for rapid communication with other regional centres, and locally, the crossing point of the river Colne at Hampermill became part of a route from Verulamium to the upper Thames. Archaeologists have found remains of a Belgic/Roman villa near Hampermill which had several phases of development before being abandoned in the fifth century A.D. Another road about two miles north of the river Colne linked Verulamium with Silchester near Reading. This roadway encouraged development of Roman villas on the western side of the river Chess, particularly at Loudwater where a substantial mill complex has recently been excavated, showing traces of deer and pig farming. Other Roman villas were most likely situated near other accessible crossing points of the local rivers, probably at Pinesfield and Micklefield. The retreat of the Romans in the mid-fourth century led to the decline of the local villa economy, particularly those like Loudwater which depended on a reliable market. The area reverted to sparsely populated woodland where subsistence farming prevailed.

The valley continued to be poorly populated even after the early invasions of the Saxons and only began to grow again in the reign of king Offa. In A.D. 796 an estate of 'five farmsteads with all its ancient bounds in the place which is called Pynnelsfeld' was granted into the ownership of the recently founded Abbey of St Alban by a charter of Egfrith, king of the Mercians. Pynnelsfeld, now Pynesfield, is situated on the river Colne, three miles downstream of the marshy confluence of the rivers, and in Saxon times was the most important farmstead in the area. There is some confusion as to how far its ancient bounds stretched but the Roman road between Verulamium and Silchester was certainly the northern boundary and on the west followed Pynesfield's own field limits. The extent of Egfriths's endowment southwards and eastwards is obscure but the most likely suspects are the river Colne to the south and eastwards the trackway along the ridge of hills above the river Gade. These limits match with the later boundaries of the northern part of the ancient parish of Rickmansworth. The lands south of the river Colne around the Saxon settlement of Batchworth had been granted to St Albans Abbey at its foundation in A.D. 793 but the areas had been used by early abbots as dowry payments for their daughters. They were only reclaimed by the abbey in the early 11th century and were added to Egfrith's endowment to become the southern portion of Rickmansworth parish.

The settlement called Rickmansworth started life in the Saxon period as a single farmstead or worth situated between the southern edge of the ridge of the Chiltern Hills and the marshy mere or lake which still surrounded the meeting place of the three rivers. Traditionally the name was thought to derive from Ricmaer's farm, but more modern thought concludes that the farm was named after its physical situation. The Old English word for ridge is 'hrycg' and for mere is 'maere', which perfectly describe the location and until the 18th century the alternative spelling of the town's name was Rickmeresworth.

In the late Saxon period a wooden chapel was erected on a gravel spur of land south of the farmstead but above the waters of the river Colne. The chapel became the religious focal point of an area of nine thousand acres stretching from Pynesfield in the west to Cassio bridge on the border of Watford parish and from Batchworth Heath in the south to Chorley Wood in the north. Both chapel and parish took the name of Rickmansworth and in time the chapel became the church of St Mary the Virgin, but since it was surrounded by water was generally known as 'Our Lady of the Island'. The parish was the southwesterly extent of the lands of St Albans Abbey which became part of the shire of Hertford in the reign of king Edgar.

As part of the land holdings of St Albans Abbey, Rickmansworth was exempt from the jurisdiction of the shire reeve and was only answerable to the Abbot of St Albans and his officials.

In late Saxon times when Leofstan was abbot of St Albans Abbey new roadways were constructed through the forest to encourage pilgrims to visit the shrine of St Alban. Such a roadway was made through the lands of Egfrith's endowment, keeping just above the winter floodline of the river Colne. This road later became part of the king's highway from St Albans to Windsor. Around this time the Abbey of St Albans defined five hides of land on the uplands of Croxley, north east of Rickmansworth, as a home farm for the abbey whose produce either directly or indirectly went to feed the abbey monks. Abbot Leofstan was of Norman origin and it was probably during his abbacy that the abbey property was divided into administrative areas called manors in the Norman fashion. As with the parish, the manor was called Rickmansworth although there was little settlement beside the church and the farmstead.

After the conquest of England by William of Normandy in 1066 the lands of Rickmansworth parish were confirmed as being in the ownership of the Abbey of St Albans but the people of the parish lost their rights of ownership, though not their rights of usage, in the common lands of the manor. Around 1086 all the lands of Rickmansworth were recorded in the Domesday Survey for Hertfordshire. The survey showed that the lord of the Manor of Rickmansworth was the Abbot of St Albans Abbey and that there was arable land for 20 ploughs in the parish. The abbey held a quarter of the best arable land for its own use, but just over half of their allocation was cultivated whereas nearly all the arable land held by the parishioners was under the plough.

In the whole of the manor there were no more than fifty households ranging from the four families of Norman-French origin at the top of the social hierarchy to the five slaves at the bottom. The largest group were the 22 villager households who, with the families of nine smallholders and the Frenchmen, had 14 ploughs. In addition there were the households of the five cottagers who with the slaves probably worked at Croxley on the demesne land of the abbey. The one mill on the Rickmansworth manor was probably on the river Chess between Croxley and Rickmansworth and was rented out for a payment of 5s. 4d. The fishery was also rented out for four shillings and meadow land was plentiful enough for four ploughs. The livestock had plentiful pasture and there was woodland enough to feed twelve hundred pigs. Before the Norman Invasion, the value of the manor had been £20 and, although its value almost halved after 1066 due to the destruction of the invaders, twenty years later the manor had recovered and was valued at £20 10s. The hide was the taxable unit of the period and Rickmansworth manor was taxed at 15 hides.

In the early 12th century the most profitable lands in the Manor of Rickmansworth, including the demesne lands at Croxley, were granted away as knights' fees to men who provided the king's military service on behalf of the Abbey of St Albans. Lands on the Batchworth side of the river, except for the common land of Batchworth Heath, became a knights' fee property, under the lordship of the de Batchworth family who also became lords of nearby Harefield. The village of Batchworth developed under the patronage of the family and in 1269 was granted the right to hold a Charter Fair every 17 May on condition that if a year were missed the right was revoked.

The rents of the remaining tenants in the manor of Rickmansworth were assigned to the kitchen of the Abbey of St Albans. The tenants also had to supply presents to the abbey for two of the great feast days of the year—48 hens and one hog at Christmas and 1,000 eggs and a hog at Easter. The contracted lands of the manor of Rickmansworth began to develop in the 13th century under the auspices of two successive abbots of St Albans. Adjacent to the church of Rickmansworth, Abbot John of Hertford created the Bury Farm by enclosing grazing land said to be surplus to the needs of the free tenants. He applied for a grant of free warren over the lands but the tenants disputed the attempt to curtail their right of hunting over the land and took the abbot to court, but lost their case. The marshy land of the Bury Farm was drained by the digging of the Town Ditch, placing the farm buildings in a large moated enclosure, but the arable fields of the farm were across the main roadway through the parish on higher ground. It is thought that the mill at Mill End was also constructed at this time, to serve the tenantry on the western side of the manor as the Croxley mill served those to the east.

A manorial court, to supervise the running of the manor, was set up at Rickmansworth under the control of the abbey sacrist. He was the officer of the abbey to whom the care of the parish and church of Rickmansworth had been assigned in the 12th century. He also received the tithes and offerings of the church of Rickmansworth for the repair and ornamentation of St Albans Abbey.

Abbot John's successor, Abbot Roger of Norton, pursued a policy of enlarging the abbey's land holdings by purchase or exchange. Within the parish Abbot Roger acquired La Pennelonde and other small parcels of land which in 1286 were granted to the sacrist of St Albans Abbey and became the headquarters of the Manor of Rickmansworth. The 13th century also saw the wooden chapel extended into a substantial church of flint construction and, like many other churches of the time, the church was dedicated to the Virgin Mary. From the year 1270 the church attained the dignity of having its own vicar, although the Abbot of St Albans still held the position of rector. In 1349, the year of the Great Pestilence, three vicars were appointed in succession to the parish of Rickmansworth but such was the toll of the plague among the clergy that they were unable to take up their duties.

The roadway from the church joined the main road after crossing the Town Ditch and plots of land were set aside here for shops and an inn. It was probably this inn which was honoured by Edward, Prince of Wales when he was entertained in Rickmansworth in November 1292. His bill of expenses can still be seen in the Public Record Office ranging from 22s. 3d. for the dispensary and 43s. 8d. for the kitchen to 20s. 3d. for the stable and 12d. alms.

In 1363 the Manor of Rickmansworth was worth £18 4s. 9d. a year to the Abbot but over half of that was appropriated to the convent kitchen. Abbot Thomas de la Mare so adjusted the finances that the revenue of the convent's kitchen was dependent on the Bury farm, whereas his personal income came from the land rents and the profits of cattle grazing on common lands both of which could be increased at will.

A generation later tenants on the Manor of Rickmansworth, along with many other abbey tenants, felt they were being pressurised by the Abbot to revert to the former practice of services instead of money rents. They also felt the Abbot was undermining their rights of pasture on the commons, their right to fish in the local rivers, and their rights of free hunting and fowling in certain areas. It was these underlying resentments which led the men of Rickmansworth to join the uprising against the Abbot of St Albans and his officials in June 1381, which was part of widespread disaffection against manorial lords later called the Peasants' Revolt. The uprising in Hertfordshire was started by the people of St Albans to free their town from the dominance of the monastery and they summoned the representatives of the local townships to join them in their fight. The men of Rickmansworth arrived in St Albans on Saturday 15 June, the same day as the general charter from the king granting the rebels their freedoms. Recognising the inevitable, the Abbot began to issue charters to all the demanding townships.

The Rickmansworth charter granted all tenants living within the town the right to hold their tenancies 'free and of free condition'. The charter also stated that

> all the tenants of the said lands and tenements, their heirs and assigns may freely grant, sell and assign the said lands and tenements with their appurtenances, to whomsever they will, paying to the said Abbot and Convent and their successors for ever yearly the rents used and accustomed for all services and demands. And that all the aforesaid Tenants and their heirs and assigns may have free fishery in the waters called Pichelesborne to fish there, as is and was the custom, and also free common in Burymore, in Bacheworthe, with all their beasts and animals, except pigs and geese, paying yearly to the said Abbot and Convent and their successors, yearly for each head of cattle three pence for all services and demands.

This charter gave the people of Rickmansworth everything they desired and for a few days they rejoiced in their freedoms, but around the beginning of July the King recalled his letters of manumission and all the charters had to be surrendered to the Abbot and destroyed. Fortunately, enough copies had been made to cause great annoyance to

Abbot Thomas and his successors. The rebel ringleaders from each township were imprisoned but all seem to have been pardoned, and all the inhabitants of Hertfordshire between the ages of 15 and 60 had to swear fealty to King Richard in the courtyard of the Abbey of St Albans.

Despite this setback, by the early years of the 15th century all the tenants of the manor had gained several concessions, becoming customary tenants who held their lands according to the custom of the manor, enshrined in the manor court rolls, instead of at the will of the lord. Each tenant held a copy of the terms of his tenure and had also acquired the right to dispose of his personal goods by leaving a will, instead of his entire property being considered to belong to his feudal lord. The Abbey of St Albans also surrendered their rights of first refusal on any land sales within their domain giving their tenants a greater freedom to buy and sell land on the open market.

In the early 15th century an entrepreneurial and wealthy London citizen called William Flete acquired a small estate in the Batchworth area because of non payment of a debt. Over the next twenty years he built up a considerable estate by purchasing neighbouring properties including the Manor of the More, a mile and a half upstream of Rickmansworth. In 1426 he obtained a royal licence to build a small castle at the More, and to enclose 600 acres of land for parkland. The castle was built of brick and stone with crenellations, turrets and battlements and provided local opportunities of employment as the new building also necessitated the re-siting of the existing moats. The two storied castle was designed as a quadrangle enclosing the timber-framed house of the Aignel family which was later demolished. Two impressive semi-octagonal brick towers guarded the entrance where there was a drawbridge over the moat. The bricks were locally made at Woodcock Hill and Chorley Wood where small pockets of clay were found in the hills. John Flete, a relative of William's, had set up the brickworks to supply bricks for the chimneys of the royal palace at Kings Langley.

Within a few years of the death of William Flete, the More estate was leased to George Neville, Archbishop of York, who was detained there by Edward IV under house arrest before being exiled for treasonable activities. Subsequently the Manor of the More came into the King's hands and he used its profits to repair the roofs and ceilings of the State Apartments at Windsor Castle and to provide a new bay window in the Queen's great chamber there.

Cardinal Wolsey, in his rôle as Abbot of St Albans, was a later occupant of the Manor of the More, and he extended William Flete's house with galleried courtyards and also built an outer court to provide lodgings and stabling for his enormous retinue. In 1525, at the Manor of the More, Cardinal Wolsey was host to peace negotiations between England and France which resulted in the Treaty of the More being signed there on 25 August 1525. Henry VIII's first wife, Catherine of Aragon, also spent some time here when she was banished from the court for refusing to divorce the king. However, Rickmansworth proved to be too accessible for visitors from London so the Queen was soon moved further north.

While Cardinal Wolsey was living at the Manor of the More there was a terrible calamity at Rickmansworth church. One night in 1522 the church was deliberately set ablaze by Lollard sympathisers who particularly targeted the statues of the saints and the image of Christ on the rood screen. The arsonists made sure of their blaze by pushing staves of wood, wrapped in fibrous material, through the bars of the chancel and they also set fire to the reserved sacrament on the high altar. The christening font was broken up and holy water scattered about the church and in the vestry ornaments and jewels were set ablaze. The organ in the rood loft was also destroyed, helped by the 200 pounds of candle wax stored there but the church was saved from total destruction because of its flint walls.

The parishioners of Rickmansworth were very generous in bequeathing money in their wills for the repair of the church but nevertheless it took 15 years for the church to be fully restored.

The Lollards were followers of John Wycliff who believed that personal faith came from the scriptures and who therefore opposed pilgrimages, indulgences and worship of relics as a means of salvation. Consequently they were being persecuted by the established church personified in Cardinal Wolsey and the Bishop of Lincoln within whose diocese lay Rickmansworth parish. A few weeks before the fire two Lollards from nearby Amersham had been burnt at the stake on the instructions of the Bishop of Lincoln. One of the martyrs had family connections at Rickmansworth and it was assumed that local Lollards had hit back on a church with which the two prelates were connected.

After the death of Cardinal Wolsey in 1530 the control of Rickmansworth came into the King's hands, with Sir John Russell of Chenies being appointed as bailiff. At that time the dissolution of the Abbey of St Albans was not in question but six years later all the liberties granted to the Abbey of St Albans by king Edgar before the Norman Conquest were revoked. Three years later the Abbey was dissolved, severing a link with Rickmansworth which had lasted for over seven hundred years.

In 1542 the Bailiff, men and inhabitants of Rickmansworth were granted a royal licence to hold a Saturday market and a fair on the Feast of the Assumption and the people celebrated their rise to the status of townsfolk. Soon a two-storied Market Hall of timber-framed construction was built in the middle of the High Street of Rickmansworth within a stone's throw of *The Swan*, the main inn of the town. The area of the town was small, consisting of the church and Church Street and a hundred yards or so, either side of the Market Hall in the High Street. The few shops were on the northern side of the High Street as the Town Ditch was very close to the roadway on the south. The townsfolk of Rickmansworth remained under the control of the parish vestry and remained as tenants of the Manor of Rickmansworth. There were just over three hundred families within the parish and probably about fifty families in the town itself which created a good inter-dependence of community.

The open lower storey of the Market Hall had been constructed to protect the bolts of cloth of the local cloth-making industry which had started in the town in the early 16th century. The woven cloths were cleansed and thickened in the Town Ditch, then known as the Tenter Stream, then dried and stretched on tenter frames in the nearby meadow and up Tenter Hill, later Solomon's Hill. As production increased the fulling process was moved to the mills at Scotsbridge and Loudwater but the cloth was still woven in the cottages and collected by the clothiers for the later processes. The Alexander family of Scotsbridge were linked by marriage to John Palmer who from the 1520s had the tenancy of Bury Farm. John was by profession a surveyor of the royal stable, who brought an interest in the finer points of Tudor fashion to a fascinated Rickmansworth.

Tudor Rickmansworth generated a school where the young gentlemen of the town were taught the rudiments of English and Latin grammar under the direction of a Mr. Stocke. It is likely that the school met in the vestry of the church, or possibly in the Market Hall. The school was known to have been in existence around 1590, when Thomas Fotherley jnr. was a pupil there, but probably came into existence soon after the closure of the school at the Abbey of St Albans. The Rickmansworth school would seem to have foundered by the 1630s but in its prime some of the pupils went on to University. Gonville and Caius College, Cambridge had an interest in the parish as the owner of the Manor of Croxley.

Rickmansworth grew in stature under the glory of the Tudors as befitted a town with a royal manor within the parish. Henry VIII often hunted in the parkland of the Manor of the More and used the castle to house part of the extensive royal wardrobe. When the Manor of Rickmansworth was granted to the Bishop of London in 1550, little except the landlord changed and nine years later the manor was back in royal ownership. However, the Bishop of London retained the ecclesiastical rights of the parish together with the ownership of the Manor House, afterwards known as Rectory Farm, and woodland in the south of the parish still known as Bishops Wood. The Manor of Rickmansworth re-established itself on the Bury farm and a new building was erected on the farm to house the manorial court and the visiting officials of the lordship of the manor.

Sir Gilbert Wakering was a later tenant of the Bury estate, purchasing a 60-year lease from the crown in 1610 because his London-born wife refused to live on his Staffordshire estate. Reputedly, it was he who joined the two houses on the Bury estate, but more likely it was his stepson Sir John Hewitt who made the Bury into a house fit for the baronet he became.

In December 1631 the Lordship of the Manor of Rickmansworth was purchased by Thomas Fotherley whose family had lived in the parish for over a hundred years. Thomas had made his fortune during a successful career in the households of the nobility, becoming in the process a staunch supporter of Charles I. However, the Fotherleys did not live at the Bury, as the Hewitt family still had several years of their tenancy to run.

Nine years later the Civil War began and Rickmansworth was in an area controlled by the Roundhead armies. Thomas Fotherley had prudently mortgaged his lordship to provide money for King Charles and although an attempt was made to sequester the Bury Farm, Sir John Hewitt refused to compound for it on the grounds that it had belonged to his mother who had transferred it to her grandchildren.

From 1640 Rickmansworth church was in the hands of the puritans who thereby ejected the Rev. William Edmonds who had suceeded his father as vicar of the parish in the 1620s. The restoration of the monarchy and the established church in 1660 caused the puritan dissenters to withdraw to the countryside. The Society of Friends (Quakers) had a strong network of members in the secluded hills of Buckinghamshire with some meeting places across the Hertfordshire border. One of their leaders, William Penn, married Gulielma Springett at Kings Farm, Chorley Wood, and set up house in Rickmansworth for the first five years of their marriage. William Penn was the founding father of Pennsylvania where he aimed to provide a place of religious tolerance for Quakers and other nonconformists.

The years after the restoration of the monarchy were times of uncertainty for Rickmansworth. The cloth industry had not survived the demise of the Alexander and Palmer families and repeated epidemics of plague and smallpox were undermining the population. Attempts were made to solve the growing social problem by the provision of almshouses. John Beresford, who had made a fortune dealing in gunpowder in the Civil War, bequeathed two cottages on the south side of Rickmansworth High Street which were turned into almshouses for four elderly people. Thirty years later John Fotherley, who had recovered the Lordship of the Manor of Rickmansworth, though not his father's fortune, built five almshouses on the north of the High Street for five poor and needy widows. The Beresford or church almshouses were later relocated in Bury Lane whereas the Fotherley or manor almshouses remained on their original site until the 1930s.

Despite the general decline of the town, one neccessity of life, the manor brewhouse at the Gorralls, continued to succeed under the supervision of John Skidmore. Coincidentally, he also had the copyhold of the *Swan Inn* in Rickmansworth High Street.

Another brewery came to Rickmansworth in the 1720s when Samuel Salter built a malthouse on the outskirts of Rickmansworth Park, where the Catholic Church is today. His brewery works were at the eastern end of Rickmansworth High Street and the nearby

Coach and Horses public house was the brewery tap. The family connection with the brewery was maintained until 1829 and the business continued to be a dominant feature of the town for another century.

The provision of education in the town was revived in 1711 by the founding of the Rickmansworth Charity School for teaching poor children to read and instructing them in the knowledge of the Church of England. The school was funded by the subscriptions of the gentry, including nonconformists, and at first met in a rented room. In 1814 a 'House for the Charity School' was purchased but, when the Rickmansworth Poor House at the eastern end of the town was closed in 1836, the growing school moved into their former premises.

The construction of a Palladian mansion in Moor Park in 1720 brought welcome opportunities of employment to Rickmansworth. The first house in Moor Park had been built by the 3rd Earl of Bedford in the 1620s although it was the Countess of Bedford's garden which excited the plaudits of the day. In 1670 the Moor Park estate was purchased by the Duke of Monmouth, the natural son of Charles II, and he built a new house higher up the hill. The house can hardly have been completed before the attempted invasion of 1685 which resulted in the execution of the Duke on Tower Hill.

Benjamin Hoskyn Styles purchased the house in 1720 with the proceeds of his insider dealing in the South Sea Company. Mr. Styles and his architect, Sir James Thornhill, extended Monmouth's fine brick house and covered the whole building in Portland stone, which had to be transported by river and road from Dorset. Inside, the entrance hall had its ceiling removed to make an imposing reception room surmounted by a flat ceiling painted to look like an Italian dome. Styles spent £150,000 on the house but Sir James had to go to law to get his bills paid. The extravagant house continued as a source of local employment as successive wealthy owners imposed their own ideas on the estate. Other more modest houses were built at Moneyhill and in Rickmansworth Park where Henry Fotherley Whitfield created a smaller version of the Moor Park mansion.

The Industrial Revolution of the 18th century brought about an increasing demand for paper and Rickmansworth mills were revitalised for paper production, eventually making Rickmansworth the foremost paper-making town in Hertfordshire. The first paper mill in the parish of Rickmansworth was at Soles Mill, on the river Chess, which started production in 1746. Ten years later, two former fulling mills at Loudwater and Scotsbridge as well as the mill at Mill End had all changed over to paper production. On the river Colne, Batchworth had two mills on the same premises, one for paper and one for corn. The Rickmansworth mills continued to make hand-made paper until the 1880s with Loudwater and Scotsbridge Mills becoming famous for supplying paper for the *Illustrated London News*, owned by Herbert Ingram. The introduction of chlorine into the paper-making process allowed materials other than rags, such as esparto grass and wood pulp, to be used in the paper-making process. Adversely, a leakage of chlorine effluent into the river Chess was responsible for the closure of both the Loudwater and Scotsbridge mills. Around 1806 a new steam-powered mill was built in Rickmansworth High Street for spinning silk. The manufactory was owned by William Harty, son-in-law of Pierre Paumier of Rookery Mill, Watford and both mills were later bought by Thomas Rock Shute. The Rickmansworth Silk Mill lasted until 1889 and was sold to the Springwell Mineral Water Company, which occupied the site for another hundred years.

The most successful mill in Rickmansworth parish was the Croxley Mill on the river Gade, built by John Dickinson in 1830. Relying on machinery from the outset, the output of the mill reached 18 tons of paper per week some eight years after its opening and by 1894 production had reached 140 tons per week, taking the trade name of 'Croxley Script' around the world.

Croxley Mill was an early user of the Grand Junction Canal, which reached Rickmansworth in 1796. Since the mid-17th century there had been plans to use the local rivers to provide London with more water and around 1778 the river Colne was made navigable between Croxley and Rickmansworth. The Grand Junction Canal opened a through route to London and the Midlands with the immediate benefit of halving the local price of coal. Gradually local businesses started using the new waterway especially when Salter's Brewery constructed a side arm off the main canal to a wharf in the town. In the early 20th century the W.H. Walker & Bros. Ltd. boat-building firm set up business at Batchworth and the village developed a community to serve the canal people. Another arm of the canal was constructed to the Bury House, where John Taylor had a flour mill and used the canal for his deliveries.

The revival of nonconformity in the parish in the late 18th century was assisted by the complacency of the established church. Nathan Sharman would seem to have headed the Baptist movement in Rickmansworth parish between 1791 and 1816 as he registered four places of worship in Chorleywood and Croxley Green. He was also instrumental in setting up the Mill End congregation, which in 1823 built the Ebenezer Chapel in Uxbridge Road. In Rickmansworth town, the Baptist cause resulted in the High Street church being built in 1843. Methodism took root in the town in 1816, two years after a Methodist minister was preserved from death at the hands of a Rickmansworth mob. Small Wesleyan chapels were built in the surrounding hamlets of Heronsgate and West Hyde and subsequently substantial churches were erected in Rickmansworth, Croxley Green and Mill End. Roman Catholicism was officially re-introduced into Rickmansworth in 1886 by Father Henry Hardy, who for nearly twenty years nurtured the Catholic faith which was then developed further by the French order of the Augustines of the Assumption.

By the early 19th century the frequently repaired medieval church of St Mary's was in such a precarious state that it was no longer safe for holding services. After years of discussion, in 1824 the Parish Vestry agreed to borrow £6,000 from the Commission for New Churches to rebuild the parish church of Rickmansworth, apart from the tower. The church was built to accommodate at least two thousand people, the population of the parish having increased by a quarter in the twenty years since the first census. The money borrowed for the church was repayable within six years but such was the general poverty of the parish that the debt was only cleared 18 years later.

By the mid-19th century the town and parish were recovering from many years of depression. The rising population was finding work in the expanding paper-making mills which in turn were making profits for the mill owners and investors. The outlying hamlets of the parish were desirous of having their own churches and in 1845 the parish of Chorley Wood was formed, followed soon afterwards by West Hyde on 30 October 1846. As Croxley Mill prospered the hamlet of Croxley built their church in 1872 while Mill End parish was formed on 29 June 1875, the same year that Eastbury became part of the new Northwood Holy Trinity parish.

The Commissioners' Church was now too large for the town of Rickmansworth and, according to Lord Ebury, the owner of Moor Park, its architectural style left much to be desired. The churchwardens decided to rebuild St Mary's Church in the perpendicular style of its medieval forbear and the late Victorian church celebrated the centenary of its dedication in 1990.

Rickmansworth parish had the distinction of having the pioneer Chartist settlement within its area. The Chartist movement arose after the presentation to Parliament of a Charter of Rights, one of which was universal suffrage without property qualifications. The petition was received with insulting indifference, and Feargus O'Connor resolved to form a Chartist Land Company to provide property for industrial workers, by means of a lottery. Herringers Farm, between Mill End and West Hyde, was purchased in 1846 by the Chartist leader, who set out plots of between two and five acres. The settlement was named O'Connorville after its founder, with the estate roads being named after northern industrial towns. The tenants, chosen by ballot, were meant to be self-sufficient but the scheme foundered due to lack of agricultural experience, legal anomalies and the illness and subsequent death of Feargus O'Connor. There were only three original settlers left in 1858 when the O'Connorville estate was sold and Mr. W.P. Roberts, the radical Chartist lawyer, bought most of the ground rents. The village reverted to its original name and eventually became an exclusive estate for affluent commuters.

In 1852 the first railway came to Rickmansworth, connecting the town with Watford, some five miles away. The railway was seen as being of mutual benefit to both towns but Rickmansworth had no main line railway to boost its development. It was originally envisaged that the line would continue down the valley to Uxbridge but this never materialised. The Watford-Rickmansworth railway carried goods traffic as well as passengers and had a transhipment wharf to the canal beside its Rickmansworth terminus. Local watercress from the flourishing business of the Bradbery family of West Hyde was sent to London by this route. Later there was also a light railway from this line to the pumping station of the Colne Valley Water Company across the fields of Eastbury Farm. The line closed to passengers in 1952 and to goods in 1962 and now provides a walkway between the two towns.

Thirty years after the Watford-Rickmansworth railway was opened the Metropolitan Railway arrived in Rickmansworth and put the local fly stage coaches out of business. Opened in 1887, the line provided a fast and reliable half-hour journey to London and, just as the Watford-Rickmansworth railway had brought about some housing development near its Rickmansworth terminus, the Metropolitan line proved to be a stimulus for house building on the fields of Rectory Farm and along the Uxbridge Road. After the First World War and the subsequent sale of farms and estates in Chorleywood, Moneyhill and Moor Park to the Metropolitan Country Estates Ltd., development in Rickmansworth intensified. The population of the Rickmansworth area doubled between the wars and the shops of the town expanded to fulfil the needs of both the residents and the ramblers and cyclists discovering the pleasures of rural Metroland. Housing development was halted by the Second World War and after the war by the new Green Belt around London.

In 1953 the Rickmansworth Urban District Council decided to commemorate the Coronation of Queen Elizabeth II with a Grant of Arms incorporating symbols from families connected with the history of Rickmansworth. The shield of the armorial bearings is divided by a zig-zag 'dancetty' line from the Fotherley coat of arms above which are three circles or 'plates' from the arms of William Penn, with two stars representing Thomas White, a founder of Merchant Taylors' School, who was reputedly born at West Hyde. The lower portion of the shield consists of purple buds of flowers on a gold background from the arms of Dr. John Caius who endowed Gonville and Caius College with the Manor of Croxley. The crest surmounting the arms is a wheatsheaf representing Lord Ebury of Moor Park, faced with a blue lion's face from the arms of Cardinal Wolsey. The motto transcribes as 'Unless the Lord builds ...' referring to the current residential character of the ancient parish of Rickmansworth which by the 1950s had reached nearly twenty-nine thousand people.

Over the centuries Rickmansworth has grown from a small farm to a bustling community. We only know its history because previous generations have recorded their actions. If future generations are to know about life in Rickmansworth in the 20th century, then the responsibility is ours.

Church Street and Bury Lane

1. The Church of St Mary the Virgin, Church Street, 1815. The town grew around the parish church which was situated on an island site formed by the rivers Chess and Colne and the town ditch. The original chapel was enlarged or rebuilt in the early 13th century and Lollard sympathisers tried to burn the interior in the 15th century.

2. The Church of St Mary the Virgin, Church Street, pre-1890. In 1825 the medieval church was declared unsafe and, except for the tower, was demolished. The replacement church with interior galleries was designed by William Atkinson to accommodate some two thousand worshippers and cost £6,000. This was borrowed from the Commissioners for Building New Churches, the church being consecrated in September 1826.

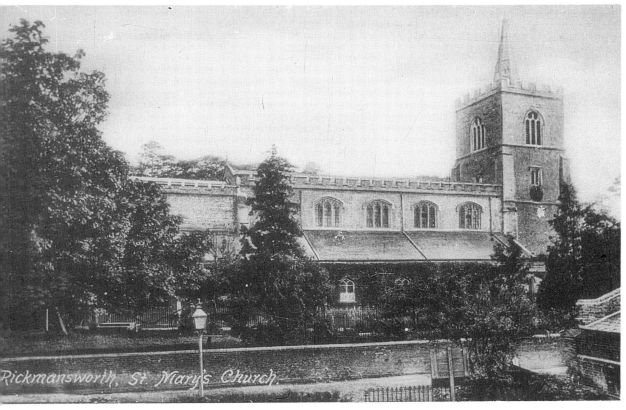

Rickmansworth, St. Mary's Church.

3 *Above*. The Priory in Church Street was originally built in the early 16th century as a church house where parish festive gatherings, such as church-ales or bride-ales, could be held. In earlier times, such gatherings were held in the parish church to raise funds for church purposes. With the rise of protestantism, such festivities were no longer held within a sacred building.

4 *Above right*. The rear of The Bury House, Bury Lane. The Bury became the manor house of Rickmansworth in 1559. Thomas Fotherley purchased the manor of Rickmansworth in 1631 but could not live in it as it was leased to Sir Gilbert Wakering's family who improved the property. Later Fotherleys and Fotherley-Whitfields lived at The Bury until 1786 when they built Rickmansworth Park House.

5 *Right*. The front of The Bury House, Bury Lane. A century later John Taylor had a flourishing flour mill at The Bury and, when he died in 1869, Lord Ebury purchased the property. It was purchased by Hertfordshire County Council in 1936 and was used as a civil defence centre during the Second World War.

6 The Watersplash, Bury Lane, *c.*1912. Until 1799, this was a private roadway but in that year Henry Fotherley-Whitfield gave the right-of-way to the town on condition that it maintained the footbridge to the side of the ford. This photograph by Tom Harris shows his baby sister Eva, his sister Doris (in white), and their cousin Lena Lasdale.

7 The Watersplash, Bury Lane, *c.*1950. As far back as 1909 there were proposals for culverting the ford but these were dropped because of local protests. In the hard winter of 1963, the ford froze and Bury Lane had to be closed, giving the council the impetus for culverting the splash. The ditch alongside Bury Lane was culverted in 1939.

8 The Rickmansworth Town Band outside Ebury Hall, Bury Lane, *c.*1909. The brass band used to play in the High Street every Saturday night, and on Sunday mornings it would accompany the hymn singers in St Mary's Church. Ebury Hall was formerly a straw plaiting factory, producing covers for wine bottles.

9 The platform at Church Street Station. The station was opposite St Mary's Church. At first, the line was in private ownership with the L.N.W.R. running the mixed passenger and freight trains. The line was sold to the L.N.W.R. in 1881, transferred to the L.M.S. in 1923, electrified in 1927, closed to passengers in March 1952 and freight in 1967.

10 Church Row Cottages (Physic Row), Church Street. These Georgian or early Victorian cottages were sideways to the road adjoining Church Terrace, opposite St Mary's Church. There were 12 small back-to-back dwellings but in later years the two cottages nearest the road were made into one. Demolished in 1965, the Skidmore Way clinic is now on the site.

11 St Mary's Church and *The Feathers*, Church Street. In 1878 the public house was known as *The Cock* and the earliest known reference to the pub is 1780 when it was bought by Stephen Salter. In early Victorian times, the inn enjoyed the privilege of supplying refreshments in the churchyard between morning and evening services to worshippers at the parish church.

12 *Above left*. Floods in Church Street in 1947. During the floods about 350 houses in Talbot Road, Norfolk Road and Church Street were flooded to a depth of 18 inches. Flooding here was not unusual and the council frequently pressed carts and charabancs into emergency use. Worley Son & Lindsay, builders, occupied the corner premises of Norfolk Road.

13 *Left*. The Victoria Fish Supply at 28 Church Street, 1912. In the 1930s, Boyd's served celebrated fish and chip suppers to the large crowds who came to the Aquadrome. The shop remained a fish shop until the 1980s when it moved to the old fire station premises in the High Street.

14 *Above*. Church Street at the junction with Bury Lane, *c*.1900. John Jones the coachmaker moved here when his workshop in the High Street burned down in 1855 and his business developed into motor vehicles. Next door was William King the greengrocer and Went the confectioner. Across the road was Cook's the grocer and the *Kings Arms* public house, closed in 1977.

15 The Chequers Tea Rooms, Church Street, was a public house until 1912. It lost its licence one memorable day that year when 12 inns were closed down by the local licensing justices. It then became a tea room and later a restaurant. Rowley the photographer moved here in 1958, occupying the premises vacated by the Zerny Engineering Company.

16 Church Street at the junction with Talbot Road, *c.*1900. On the extreme left of the picture is Beeson & Sons the ironmongers and opposite is the ironmongery firm of Davis. To the right is Vicarage Bridge, which crosses the Town Ditch adjoining Marble Arch Cottages. The cottages were demolished in 1910 because of their insanitary state and overcrowding.

17 Royal Artillery church parade, Church Street, 1915. The third London Brigade was stationed in Rickmansworth from March to May 1915. The officers were based in the council offices in Church Street while the men were billeted around the town. The guns and horses were quartered at Rickmansworth Park. In the background is the small shop of William Taylor which sold tobacco and fishing tackle.

18 The Vicarage in Church Street, 1970. The nucleus is late medieval and, like other neighbouring properties, the ground floor is below street level. There is an overhanging oriel window on the first floor and the gables are picturesque. The building has been rebuilt and extended many times over the centuries.

19 Colour Corner on the junction of Church Street and the High Street. When Barclays Bank moved to Church Street in 1899, the vicarage wall and bank site were moved back to widen the road. There are now traffic lights at this junction. Colour Corner moved here in the 1950s. It has now gone as have London Kiosks and Dewhursts.

High Street

20 Salter's Brewery in the High Street, *c.*1926. Samuel Salter opened a brewery at the eastern end of the High Street in the early 18th century and bought his first public house, the nearby *Coach and Horses*, in 1741. The Cannon Brewery of Clerkenwell purchased Salter's in 1920 and the brewery buildings were demolished in 1972. Alfred Walker is the gentleman in the picture.

21 *Above left.* The Picture House, High Street, was Rickmansworth's second cinema and the first purpose-built one. It opened on 12 March 1927 on part of Salter's Brewery site which was then owned by Walker Bros. It could seat 504 people in the stalls and 173 in the balcony and included a spacious ballroom and tea lounge. The cinema closed in June 1963.

22 *Left.* On the Dust—Messrs. G. Cornwall and W. Rivett outside the Picture House, High Street, 1927. F.G. Hall of Frogmoor was the local contractor employed by the council in 1927 to collect refuse. Godfrey and Bill were known as the singing dustmen because they would sing and dress up for special occasions. On election days, it was 'vote for Lord Dusty'.

23 *Above.* The Elms, High Street, 1964. This red-brick house was built *c.*1725 and is noted for being the summer residence of George Eliot (Mary Ann Evans) in 1875 where she worked on her novel *Daniel Deronda*. The convent and school of St Joan of Arc was established here in 1922.

24 The Wesleyan Chapel, High Street, 1897. The chapel was built at a cost of £2,500 and opened in 1866. The site had originally housed a smaller chapel and the coachbuilding firm of a Mr. Jones, but both properties were destroyed by fire in 1855, and the church subsequently bought the site. Benson, who made the church clock (and Big Ben), spent his childhood in Mill End.

5 High Street (East). On the left is the *Coach and Horses*, bought by Salter's in 1741 as their brewery tap. The barn at the rear was registered as a meeting place for the Baptist community in 1802. At the end of the cottages on the right was a bakery owned by Mrs. Gristwood, later taken over by the Nobbs family.

6 Redpale House in High Street was originally an integral medieval wattle and daub house. It was owned in the 17th century by Rowland Beresford, whose father had built the Beresford Almshouses. The house, on the the corner of Talbot Road, was subdivided into two dwellings in the 19th century and, later again, into four. Sometimes referred to as Basing Manor, the building was demolished in 1966.

27 The National School, High Street. The former Rickmansworth Poor House was converted in 1836 into a school with segregated classes for boys and girls— divided by a heavy felt double curtain. It was extended as a National School in 1851. Shortly after the school closed in 1936 the premises were let to the Siegwart Floor Company.

28 The Baptist Chapel, High Street, was consecrated in 1843 and was built at a cost of £800. It recently celebrated its 150th anniversary. The Rev. R. Bayne, minister here from 1865 to 1871, wrote *The History of Rickmansworth and Surrounding Parishes.*

29 James Peddle, funeral furnisher, High Street. Peddle started as a builder in Station Road but on moving to these premises he added funeral services to his business as Chilton the undertaker had ceased trading. When these cottages were demolished, the business moved into the replacement offices. The empty site is the former *Prince of Wales* public house which closed in 1912.

30 Basing House, High Street. William Penn lived in a house on this site following his marriage on 4 April 1672. The house was later refronted or possibly rebuilt in 1740, while side wings were added during the occupancy of Dr. Roderick Henderson who lived here from 1870 until his death in 1929. Rickmansworth Council purchased his house in 1930 for council offices.

HERE WILLIAM PENN (1644 – 1718)
QUAKER STATESMAN AND MAN OF VISION,
FOUNDER OF PENNSYLVANIA AND PLANNER
OF PHILADELPHIA, FRIEND OF THE INDIANS,
CRUSADER FOR CIVIL AND RELIGIOUS LIBERTY,
DESIGNER OF EUROPEAN PEACE, RESIDED FOR
FIVE YEARS AFTER HIS MARRIAGE TO
GULIELMA MARIA SPRINGETT (1644 – 1694)
THE STONE ABOVE THIS TABLET FROM PENNSBURY
PENNSYLVANIA, THE ANCIENT HOME OF
WILLIAM PENN ON THE DELAWARE RIVER,
WAS PRESENTED BY THE PENNSYLVANIA
HISTORICAL AND MUSEUM COMMISSION WHO
ARE THE CUSTODIANS OF THE PROPERTY.

31 Unveiling a plaque to William Penn at Basing House, High Street, 1951. The plaque, at the entrance to the house, was provided by the Pennsylvania Historical and Museum Commission as a memorial to William Penn's residence here. The stone comes from Penn's house on the bank of the Delaware river in Pennsylvania.

32 Ottawa and Basing Cottage fronted the High Street and were adjacent to the grounds of Basing House. Ottawa remained in private hands while Basing Cottage was occupied by Catholic pupils taught by nuns of the Order of the Daughters of Jesus, later transferring to become St Joan of Arc School. Rickmansworth Library now occupies the site.

OTTAWA

33 W. Palmer, provision merchant, High Street. John Palmer originally occupied the shop in 1861 but by 1891 Mrs. Leticia Palmer was running the business, by which point she had also become a wine merchant. William Palmer took over in the late 1920s and the business was sold to Frank Dickins in 1949.

34 F.L. Dickins, family grocer, High Street. Frank Dickins came to Rickmansworth in 1932 as manager for Cullen's when that grocery company bought the long established Dalton's shop. Dickins purchased Palmer's in 1949 and set himself up as a general provisioner and wine and spirit merchant. The provision side of the business was closed in 1971.

35 'May they be Happy', High Street. This triumphal arch was erected in the High Street between Johnson's Corner and *The Bell* public house (opposite Church Street). It celebrated the marriage of the eldest son of the 1st Lord Ebury, the Hon. Robert Wellesley Grosvenor, to the Hon. Emily Beaujolais on 20 May 1897. Note the fair in the background.

36 Johnson's Corner, High Street, 1900. In 1914 the site was purchased by Rickmansworth Council. When the council moved to Basing House in 1930 it sold Johnson's Corner to Odeon Theatres Ltd. which opened a cinema here in 1936. The company also built a row of shops that it named Odeon Parade.

37 High Street and the corner of Church Street in 1963. On the left of the picture is W.H. Cullen who took over from F. Dalton, grocer and provision merchant, who was there in 1898. In the middle of the picture is Johnson's Corner, now known as Wheatley's Corner, built in 1932. Odeon Parade is its official name, from the cinema that adjoins it.

38 Market Hall, High Street, from a painting by Absolam Evans of the Royal Society of Arts. The hall was constructed soon after the market charter of 1542 and was a timber-framed construction about 18ft. wide and 20ft. high built on 6ft. timber baulks or uprights. It was sited in the middle of the roadway—a feature which would later impede the flow of traffic.

39 Market Hall, High Street, 1864. In 1805, the Market Hall was moved to a new site at the side of the street, in line with the shops. Public subscription raised the removal cost of £115 and £260 for the purchase of the new site. Stalls were banned from the street except in the vicinity of the hall.

40 The *Swan Hotel*, High Street, 1911. The earliest recorded date for this business is 1659 when it was granted an additional licence to sell wines. The Skidmore family owned it from *c*.1692 until 1820 when their brewhouse in Goral Mead closed. Being the town's favourite venue for functions and dinners, there was public concern over its demolition in 1964.

41 Town Hall and High Street, *c.*1912. The Town Hall was erected in 1869 on the site of the former Market Hall by the Rickmansworth Town Hall Company. The hall catered for balls, dances, concerts, lectures, etc., but the most popular events were the monthly meetings of the Penny Reading Society, founded by the headmaster of the National School.

2 High Street, c.1960. The grapes are missing from *The Swan*'s pub sign and the Morris Minor shows the direction of the one-way system. Dewhurst's has yet to move; Walton's fruiterers occupies the Town Hall entrance; and Waitrose occupies the premises of Kingham's grocers. Further down the street is Carr's the ironmongery.

3 The Post Office, High Street, moved from the corner of the High Street and Church Street to these purpose-built premises in 1910. Although there was an imposing doorway, the entrance was via a side alley. The present post office was built in 1972 in place of the previous one.

44 Proclamation of King George V on 13 May 1910, High Street. The proclamation was read at a gathering of church and civic dignitaries outside the premises of Johnson & Son, general drapers. The entrance to the offices of Rickmansworth Council is to the right, just out of shot of this photograph.

45 The Post Office, High Street, 1897. Josiah Crawley, linen draper, was also postmaster at the corner of Church Street. Upon his death, his wife Amelia ran the business. The small shop between Crawley's and the Town Hall was occupied by Percy Gatehouse, harness and saddle maker.

46 *Above. The Bell* public house, High Street, 1911. The pub was of a half-timbered construction, owned by Joseph Skidmore. It was closed in the purge of 1919 and early 17th-century wall paintings were found in an upper room when demolition took place. A Charley box was sited between *The Bell* and *The George* pubs, for use by the town's watchman.

47 *Above right.* Swannell & Sly, estate agents, High Street, *c.*1960. The former *Bell* pub was let in 1919 to J.T. Sly, auctioneer. In 1900, he had bought the business of Mr. W.H. Swannell whose family had been auctioneers and estate agents in the town since 1880 or earlier. When Swannell and Sly's was demolished in 1966, the firm moved to the old police station.

48 *Right.* H.A. Saunders Ltd., High Street, 1964. Mrs. Jones established a sports and toy shop in part of her late husband's garage, later acquired by H.A. Saunders. In 1966 she sold the business to Rickmansworth Sports & Toys which, under its new owner, Mrs. Kay Mendelssohn, moved to the former Macfisheries shop when the garage was demolished.

49 Ward's Wholesale & Retail Boot Market. John Ward started his business in these premises in 1830, his family living above the shop. To the rear of the shop were workshops where he manufactured on a large scale. His best lines were thigh boots for the local watercress growers and strong hobnail boots for labourers and gravel diggers.

50 H.P. Tyler's boot shop in the High Street, 1912. Tyler bought the business from Ward's prior to 1912 and installed Mr. Egan who came from their Ramsgate shop as manager. The trademark Wellington boot which hung above the shop entrance was broken when the shop was being demolished after it had closed in August 1966.

51 Rickmansworth Electric Picture Playhouse. The Town Hall Company obtained a licence in 1906 for stage plays and a cinema licence in 1911 when it became the Picture Playhouse and began to show silent films. When the Picture House was built at the east end of High Street, the licence here was not renewed. The company was wound up in 1929.

52 *Above left*. Patterson's linen drapery, High Street, 1904. Samuel Chivers had a linen drapery here from 1854 until 1883. His son-in-law, Mr. Mungo Patterson, took over the business but, sadly, he died at the early age of 37 from pneumonia which he caught while working as a volunteer fireman, leaving three young children. His funeral cortège included the fire engine.

53 *Left*. Shops in the High Street in the 1950s. The new shops occupying the site of the Old House include Lloyds Bank, Achille Serre, Gerrard's the fruiterers and the Fifty Shilling Tailors. The latter had a prime position with windows so large that they were shattered during the war by the blast from a bomb which exploded in Croxley Green, two miles away.

54 *Above*. Boots the Chemist and W.H. Smith & Sons Ltd., High Street, in the 1960s. Boots occupied the premises of Paine's furniture shop and Rickmansworth Electrics took over Jones's radio shop next door, which later became Parrott's the wool shop. Smiths moved into this new building, with Ebury Chambers above, from its former premises next door to the Fotherley Almshouses.

55 *Above left*. Shops in the High Street in the 1960s. Rickmansworth Electrics and the Midland Bank moved into these premises in the early 1960s taking over the premises of Burton Montague Ltd., who had replaced the Metropolitan Railway Surplus Lands Company office. In the distance are the premises of E.H. Nelson who acquired Patterson's drapery *c*.1900 and stayed until 1972.

56 *Above right*. The fruit and vegetable stall of A. Lewis, at the junction of High Street and Solomon's Hill. By the early 1960s, the stall had moved into a shop directly opposite, next door to the Midland Bank, trading as Mick's Fruiterers.

57 *Below*. The Old House, High Street, pre-1938. Dr. Arthur Clarke, physician and surgeon, was the last occupant of this house before it was demolished in 1938. It had been a doctor's house and surgery since 1900 and had extensive grounds, including tennis courts, the land sloping up towards the railway, parallel with Solomon's Hill.

58 High Street at the junction with Bury Lane, 1935. Looking from Bury Lane, Wise the chemist's is on the right of the picture and forms part of the Old House, soon to be demolished. The balcony of Ford's and Eastman's is no longer there while Tesco's can be seen in the distance. On the extreme left is a branch of the Home & Colonial which had just washed its pavement.

59 The *Cart and Horses* public house, High Street. On the corner of Bury Lane, this Salter's pub was built *c.*1740 and closed down in January 1964. The set of windows was saved by the Rickmansworth Historical Society and now forms part of a set piece in the Watford Museum.

60 F.W. Gilham, boot and shoe manufacturers, High Street, 1965. The family business was established in 1870 and was still trading 100 years later. Tottering piles of shoe boxes, in every corner, greeted the customer but Edgar Gilham knew exactly where everything was. Lord and Lady Ebury were customers—but they, of course, had personal visits.

61 The picture shows the one-way traffic system operating in both portions of the High Street and lights at the junction with Station Road. The gas showroom came here in the early 1960s and is now Halfords. The International Tea Stores date from the 1920s.

62 The London and County Bank, High Street, was built in 1890 and is seen here decorated for the coronation of Edward VII and Queen Alexandra. The bank later became the Westminster.

63 The Fotherley Alms-houses, High Street, *c.*1912. John Fotherley, Lord of the Manor of Rickmansworth, built these almshouses in 1682 for five poor widows. They were later conveyed to trustees with £10 per annum to keep them in repair, the income coming from property in the parish including the Market Hall.

64 F.W. Woolworth & Co. Ltd., High Street, 1965. This shop was built on the site of the Fotherley Alms-houses and opened in 1933. The store had gas lighting, a wooden floor and polished counters. It remained here until 1971, at which point a supermarket took over the premises.

55 The High Street at the junction of Station Road, 1878. The *Sugar Loaves* public house on the left in this picture had its licence transferred to the *Victoria Hotel* and the *Queen's Arms* lost its licence in 1912. On the corner of Station Road is the *Foresters Arms* public house, later occupied by a motor and cycle repair shop and in the 1930s by Tesco Stores Ltd.

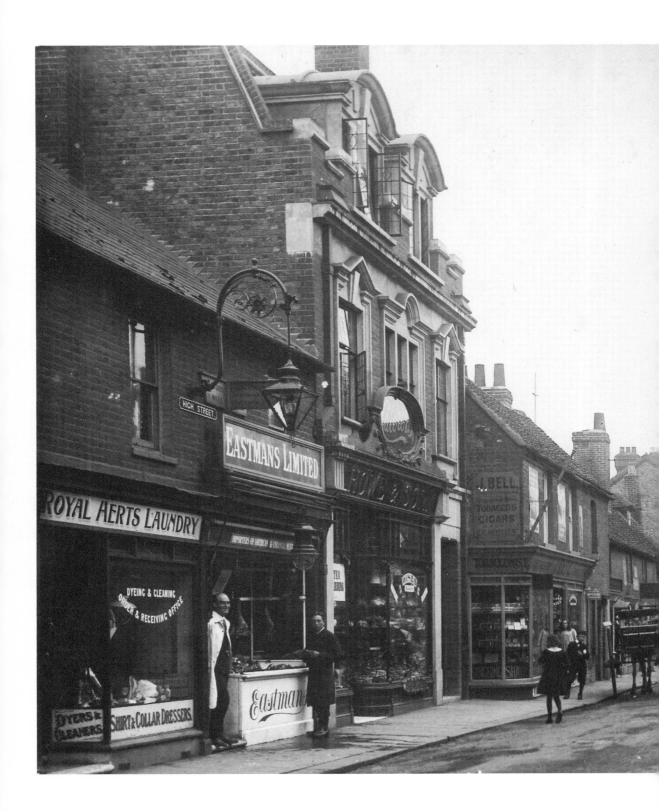

66 The High Street at the junction with Station Road, 1912. On the left of this picture is the Royal Herts Laundry receiving office and Eastman's the butcher's. Both shops were later occupied by the National Provincial Bank. In the distance is the police station, built in 1897 on the site of the Beresford Almshouses, and adjoining the fire station.

67 *Left*. The High Street from the junction with Station Road in the late 1950s. In the days of two-way traffic and schoolgirl cyclists, F.W. Woolworth still reigns supreme. Fletcher's the butcher's was shortly to be taken over by Mr. Hammett, also a butcher. In turn he was bought out by J.H. Dewhurst, which moved from the other end of the High Street. The awning is that of the Croxley Co-op grocery adjoining Pearke's Dairies.

68 *Below Left*. The High Street from the junction with Station Road in the late 1950s. A policeman was often on point duty here, especially on Saturday nights. On the right of this picture, Jon's Boutique has replaced Beesley's Florist's. The shop of H.P. Farr watchmaker was here from the war until the 1960s.

69 *Below*. National Provincial Bank and Spurrier's in the 1960s. The bank moved into the town soon after the war. The shop on the right of the picture has been a bakery since 1900, firstly under Mrs. Gristwood, then Howe & Son, and then Spurrier's. Howe's shop window was smashed by a runaway horse and coal cart in the 1920s. Sadly, both horse and driver were killed.

70 Rickmansworth Fire Station, High Street, *c.*1900. The fire station was built in 1891 by Dr. Henderson of Basing House who leased it to the brigade for £8 per year. It housed a manual engine and the newly acquired steamer with caretaker's accommodation above. The plaque commemorating its opening can still be seen in the brickwork.

71 The Rickmansworth Volunteer Fire Brigade's first steam engine, Victoria. The engine was funded by public subscription and named by Lady Ebury in 1891 at a ceremony in Bury Meadows. A magnificent water jet, 120ft. in height, was demonstrated to the amazement of the onlookers, according to a report from the *Watford Observer*.

2 Commissioning the fire engine, Muriel, in 1927. In 1925 Rickmansworth council took over responsibility for the fire brigade, purchasing a new engine which they named after Mrs. Henderson. The brigade became part of the National Fire Service and was then placed under county council control. A new fire station in Rectory Road was officially opened in 1972.

73 Dr. Henderson's funeral cortège passing the fire engine house in 1930. Dr. Henderson had been instrumental in setting up the Rickmansworth Volunteer Fire Brigade (funded by subscription) in 1869 following a disastrous fire in the High Street. He was later appointed captain and was responsible for training the volunteers. The brigade honoured him by accompanying his funeral procession.

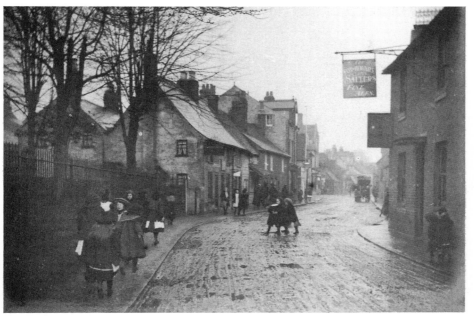

74 The *Fox and Hounds*, High Street, *c.*1905. The pub dates from the 17th century and was greatly enlarged in the 19th century. It was a Salter's pub at one time. The railings on the left are those of the Parsonage Road infants' school, opened on this site in 1854 and enlarged in 1874 to take girls up to 14 years of age. It changed from a girls' and infants' school to junior mixed infants in 1936 when the new senior school was established in Mill End.

75 Cottages in High Street (West). The *Fox and Hounds* is to the left of the man in the doorway. Charrington's coal order office is at the far end of the row of cottages adjoining the entrance to Franklin's Mineral Water Factory. The railings belong to the school.

76 Franklin's Mineral Water Factory in High Street, 1970. The old silk mill premises behind the High Street were bought by Frederick Franklin *c.*1902 when his mineral water business grew too big for the premises behind his confectionery shop in High Street. Franklin's horses were often loaned to the fire brigade to pull the engine.

77 Wensum Cottages, High Street (West), were built in 1887 and demolished in 1967-8 to make way for the new road called Wensum Way. The Rickmansworth Churches Housing Association built flats for the elderly on the remainder of the land, which were opened in 1971 by Paul Channon MP. Darrah's shop sold groceries and sweets and his photographic studio was next door.

78 The Rickmansworth war memorial at the junction of Ebury Road and Uxbridge Road, 1934. Designed by Mr. Reid Dick, it was unveiled at Ebury recreation corner in 1921 by the Earl of Cavan. With redevelopment of roads in the 1960s, the plinth was relocated to St Mary's graveyard but not the sculpture of the English lion trampling on the German eagle as it was considered inappropriate on church property.

79 Horse trough at the junction of Ebury Road with Uxbridge Road. The trough was provided by the Metropolitan Drinking Fountain Cattle Trough Association c.1880. Their name was on one side, with an exhortation on the other 'Be merciful to all God's creatures'. It was removed during the roadworks of the 1960s and is now situated at Woodoaks Farm.

Moneyhill to West Hyde

80 An aerial view of Moneyhill shows the parade of shops which has changed little since it was built in 1925. The former Cedars Stores is nearest the garage and the pedestrian crossing has been resited.

81 Two Stones Farm, Uxbridge Road. In 1856 John White, the farmer at Parsonage Farm, rented Two Stones for his working foreman. He lived there rent free but on the condition that his wife did the washing for Parsonage Farm.

82 Two Stones Cottages and the 17th-century *Halfway House*, Uxbridge Road. The cottages were built in 1914 and named The Poplars. They were unfortunately liable to flooding from the stream which crossed the Uxbridge Road and the front doors were fitted with storm boards. The name comes from the stepping stones across the ford.

83 Riverside, Moneyhill, 1905. The house was previously named Bachelor's Hall and, when David Urquart lived here, he had the first Turkish bath in England. Harvey Fellows bought the house in 1856, renaming it Riverside. He was Rickmansworth's leading attorney and an outstanding cricketer. Colin Taylor, president of the Rickmansworth Traders' Association from its inception in 1899, also lived here.

84 The Cedars, Moneyhill. Formerly known as Moneyhill, the Cedars Boarding School was established here in 1863 under its headmaster, Rev. Dr. W.F. Hurndall. Two wings were added to accommodate the students, with windows in the roof to let in light to the attic dormitories. When Hurndall retired through ill health in 1883, the premises were acquired by the Dalrymple Home for Inebriates.

85 Moneyhill Garage, Uxbridge Road, occupied a large site on the corner of Park Road and included a car showroom. A modern self-service petrol station now occupies the site.

86 Moneyhill House, Uxbridge Road. Built *c*.1722, it became known as High House to distinguish it from Moneyhill on the opposite side of the road. It was occupied at one time by Samuel Salter, the Rickmansworth brewer, and in 1881 by Mrs. Harriet Walker, a patron of St Peter's Church. York House School moved into the premises in 1950.

87 Rickmansworth Week Procession, Field Way, Mill End. The Rickmansworth Society was formed in 1953. The first Rickmansworth Week was held two years later, the opening ceremony being held at Basing House. The first Miss Rickmansworth was chosen in 1957. A procession of floats through the town heralds the start of the week, and gathers in Field Way for judging.

88 The Church of St Peter the Apostle and vicarage, Berry Lane, 1903. The church was built with flint walls in the 14th-century gothic style at a cost of £4,000 and was consecrated in 1875. The vicarage was added later, but was demolished in the 1960s and a smaller vicarage built on the same site. The surplus land was sold for housing.

89 *Left.* St Peter's School, Church Lane, in the 1930s. The buildings of the present school date from 1880. The Mill End National School for Girls and Infants was opened on 27 July 1874 with 25 pupils but from August they also admitted boys. Since 1936 this has been a junior mixed infants school administered by the church.

90 *Below left.* Shepherd's Farm, Mill End. A rear view of the garden side of the farmhouse shows its early construction. The farm is a place of pilgrimage for descendants of the three sons of James Lane who emigrated to America in 1642. Express Dairies now occupy the site of the farm buildings and the farmland has been redeveloped with houses.

91 *Below.* River Colne, Mill End, *c.*1912, showing the bridge across the Colne on the right-of-way from Mill End to Stocker's Farm. Travellers could always cross the ford but the bridge fell into disrepair and was only replaced in the early 1980s.

92 Ebenezer Chapel in Uxbridge Road, Mill End. The Mill End Baptist Church, formed in 1799, built the Ebenezer Chapel in 1823 with an extension about forty years later. After the Second World War the congregation moved to new premises in Field Way.

93 *The Vine* public house in Uxbridge Road, Mill End was opposite the *Rose and Crown*, at the bottom of Church Lane, and sold Watford Ales. On the other side of the main road was Horwood's; their sign advertising steam rollers for hire can be seen. The Ebenezer Chapel is in the background.

94 One of Horwood's wagonettes in Mill End.

95 The *Rose and Crown* in Uxbridge Road, Mill End. Invariably referred to as *The Tree*, because of the large tree in its courtyard, the pub was bought in 1767 by the Rickmansworth brewer Samuel Salter. The earliest known reference to the building dates from 1750 when it had stabling for two horses.

96 The shops and garage in Uxbridge Road, Mill End. Charlie Garrett started selling petrol in 1929 when the cost was 1s. 4d. a gallon and the garage had a 15ft frontage. By 1979 he had taken over nearby premises and had a 300ft. frontage. The car showroom was once a glove factory and during conversion, many cotton reels and pearl buttons were found.

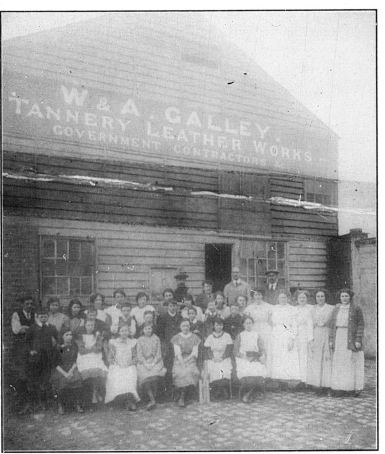

97 W. & A. Galley Tannery Leather Works, Mill End. The Wild family had held the tannery business from the 1850s. By 1914 the business had passed to the two Galley brothers who were boot and legging manufacturers and were also contractors to the army.

98 *The Plough* public house in Uxbridge Road, Mill End, pre-1912. *The Plough* stood nearly opposite the Royal Herts Laundry and to enter the pub one had to climb up two steps at the entrance to keep out flood waters. It became a private house after it was closed down in the purge of 1912. A greengrocer had the yard at the side of the pub and the mill chimney can be seen to the right of this photograph.

99 Long Lane Farm, Uxbridge Road, Mill End. The farm was small in acreage and there was a tea room in th farmhouse in the 1940s. The buildings were demolished in 1964 and the land is now farmed by the adjoinin Woodoaks Farm.

100 Drayton Ford, Mill End, pre-1912. There are two fords here, one being bridged in 1912 and the other on culverted. In 1923 a new road bridge was built and the road levelled, probably to assist the lorries of the Springwel Mineral Water Company.

101 Colne Valley Sewerage Works, Maple Cross. The prime mover behind this great undertaking was Albert Freeman, surveyor to Rickmansworth Council. Construction began in 1937 but stopped during the Second World War, restarting in 1945. Special permission was given to employ 500 prisoners of war. The works were officially opened on 23 May 1952 prior to repatriation.

02 Maple Cross shops and the Old Berkeley Hunt, meeting here probably around 1910. The hunt had local kennels n Dog Kennel Lane at Chorleywood, having moved there from Parsonage Farm around 1880. The trees are an xcellent example of the art of topiary.

103 Maple Cross shops, *c.*1950. Denham Way was constructed in the 1920s as a bypass for the narrow Uxbridge Road through West Hyde. *The Cross* public house was a Salter's pub by 1839 and had a smithy next door. Shops now occupy the site of the former cottages, called The Yews, but the trees still stand.

104 West Hyde Vicarage, *c.*1888. The vicarage was built on two acres of land belonging to Maple Lodge Farm and donated by Lord Robert Grosvenor. Parish meetings were held in the vicarage including those of the Mothers' Union, pictured here in the garden. It was sold in October 1942 and became a private house.

105 Lynster's Farm, West Hyde. Parts of the house date from 1403 when Robert Lynster was tenant but it was substantially rebuilt in the 16th century by John Beresford. In 1520, the farm was owned by the Masters of Savoy Hospital and 13 years later it was granted to St Thomas' Hospital, London.

106 Old School House, West Hyde. The firs school in West Hyde was built in 1862, enlarge in 1874 and possibly again in 1901. It wa maintained by the church but was called th West Hyde National School as it received grant from the National Society. Pupils moved acros the road to the new West Hyde County Counci School in May 1914.

107 May Cottage, West Hyde. The cottage i the oldest house in the village, probably datin from the 1650s, and is a timber-framed buildin with 4½ ins. thick walls. The exterior chimne stack had a Dutch oven built into it. Miss France Titmass lived here in 1841 and ran a penny-a week dame school before the village school wa built.

08 Royal Exchange Cottages, West Hyde, 1965, shortly before demolition. The cottages were built around 1815 and may have been constructed for workers at The Mines Royal Copper Mills towards Harefield. Twenty-nine families lived here in 1817. At one end of the terrace was the *Greyhound* pub, now a private house, and at the other the *Royal Oak*.

109 Methodist chapel and Pleasant Place Cottages, West Hyde. The cottages were probably built about 1783. The first dissenting meeting house in West Hyde dates from 1814 but this Methodist chapel was built in 1875 by Billy Saunders, the baker, in his front garden. Services were held there until 1912 when it became a fish and chip shop.

110 Richard Bradbery, watercress grower, West Hyde. William Bradbery introduced watercress to West Hyde in the early 19th century and he soon had five acres of watercress under cultivation. Richard, who inherited the firm, lived at Corner Hall and was a watercress grower and a market gardener. The watercress firm of Sansom & Sons took over the beds in 1927.

111 Harvesting watercress in West Hyde. Watercress beds are shallow, with planting or sowing carried out in June. Five to eight weeks later, the cress is ready for cutting at water level, and bunching and packing into baskets called chips. There are three-dozen bunches to each chip and, in their prime, the West Hyde beds filled some 4,000 chips every year.

Heronsgate

112 Rose Cottage, Heronsgate. In 1846 Feargus O'Connor began to construct this first Chartist settlement on the fields of Heronsgate Farm, providing small holdings, each with a two-storey house. Plot 26 was allocated to Martin Griffiths of Worcestershire. He was one of the original allottees and his family was one of very few to stay and farm the land successfully.

113 The Grange and St John's Church, Heronsgate. Plot 18 on the O'Connorville layout was for the school, built for £500 and opened in 1848. It became Heronsgate House, where Mr. J.P. Roberts the radical Chartist lawyer lived, and later a private house called The Grange. St John's Church had its origins as the chapel for Heronsgate school.

114 Wesleyan chapel, Heronsgate. The chapel was built at the instigation of Mr. John Proctor of Woodoaks Farm. The Rev. William Hirst of Poplar preached the opening sermon in December 1884 and about one hundred people attended the public tea which followed. Since its closure, the former chapel has become the village hall.

115 Heronsgate post office, 1904. This was a sub-post office to Chorleywood in 1899, as well as a grocery. By 1914, the sub-office was combined with a sweetshop.

Rickmansworth to Chorley Wood

116 Barclay & Co. Ltd., Station Road. The bank was in these temporary premises while their present bank was being built in Church Street; it moved there in 1899. The window box flowers add to the letters on either side denoting Victoria's Diamond Jubilee.

117 The Artists' Rest Home (and Auxiliary Hospital), 1914-18. The artists' home was built by F.W. Reckitt, manufacturer of starch and the famous blue whitener, and it was dedicated to the convalescence of male members of the St John's Wood Art Club whose private means were insufficient to pay the charges of private nursing homes.

118 *Right*. Rickmansworth cycle parade, Station Approach. A cycle parade pictured on the approach road to the Metropolitan Railway Station, by the Homestead, on 26 August 1908.

119 *Below*. The Homestead, Station Road. The bailiff to the Rickmansworth Park Estate lived in the house before Rickmansworth bypass decimated its grounds. Its last occupant was Mr. Pullen, the gardener to Rickmansworth council, who made Basing Gardens such a delightful haven.

120 *Below right*. Rickmansworth Metropolitan Railway Station. The Metropolitan Railway came to Rickmansworth in 1887, putting the local stage coach service to London out of business. The railway provided a fast and reliable half-hourly service to its main station at Baker Street. The development of residential estates by the railway company led to the promotion of gracious living out in the countryside in Metroland.

NUG-1903. *A.f.C. Blades.*

121 Rickmansworth Metropolitan Railway Station on the last day of steam. The railway was electrified as far as Rickmansworth in 1925, steam trains taking over for the remainder of the journey. The line was fully electrified in 1961, the last steam train running on 9 September. Enormous crowds came to witness this event and were allowed to retain their tickets as souvenirs.

122 The *Victoria Hotel*, Rectory Road. Douglas Villa was the first house opposite the newly opened railway station and it was converted into a large hotel. To provide a licence, the licence of the *Sugar Loaves* public house in the High Street was rescinded and re-issued to the *Victoria* in 1888.

123 Parsonage Farm, Rectory Road, was the manor house of Rickmansworth until 1559 when Elizabeth I divided the manor into lay and ecclesiastical property and the farm became the home farm of the Rectory Manor. John White was farmer here for much of the 19th century and land for Chorleywood Road Cemetery and Parsonage Road School was taken from the farm.

124 The Rickmansworth bypass was opened in 1934 and formed a crossroads with Station Road, Chorleywood Road and Rectory Road. On the left is the Homestead car park. The road was widened in 1969.

125 *Left*. Rickmansworth Park House was built in 1786 by Henry Fotherley Whitfield in parkland belonging to the Bury Estate. The Rickmansworth Park Estate was purchased by the Masons in 1926 in order to build a girls' school; 20 acres of parkland were given to the town as compensation for the loss of rights-of-way.

126 *Right*. The Royal Masonic School for Girls. These impressive school buildings were ready by April 1934 and officially opened by HM Queen Mary on 27 June 1934. The ceremony was attended by some five thousand brethren and their wives.

127 Loudwater House dates from *c*.1825 and Panmure Gordon, who became the owner in the 1890s, built a coach-house which became Loudwater bus garage. He maintained a herd of deer and a few kangaroos. Cameron Jeffs purchased Loudwater House in the 1920s, converting the house into flats, and later buying the rest of the estate.

128 Christ Church, Chorley Wood, 1897. The first church on this site was consecrated in 1845 and was built in the Early English style. It was demolished in 1869 and a larger church, built in restrained Gothic style, was consecrated in December 1869. The tower of the original church had been retained and was strengthened before the graceful spire was added in 1881.

129 Chorley Wood Common and The Cedars. In 1860 John Saunders Gilliat, a merchant of the City of London, bought The Cedars, Chorleywood, and rebuilt the house in the French Renaissance style. The mansion and grounds were gifted to the National Institute for the Blind in 1917 and the manorial rights of the common were given to Chorleywood council in 1921.

Rickmansworth to Croxley Green

130 Wright's Park Garage Service Station, Park Road, c.1940. The original building was erected in 1922 by the Rickmansworth & District Omnibus Company as a bus garage. It was later acquired by Harry Wright who built up a haulage and garage business. This was the proposed site for the Metropolitan Railway Station.

131 Our Lady Help of Christians Catholic Church and Presbytery, Park Road. The church was opened in 1909 and is built of concrete faced with field flints, in the early Perpendicular style. The church was enlarged in 1935 by the erection of the lady chapel and two classrooms which meant that St Monica's School could move out of its corrugated iron hut.

132 Excavating gravel in Park Road, 1886. These men are excavating near Fortune Common, prior to the coming of the Metropolitan Railway, on a site later occupied by the rear of Wright's garage. The malting house to the left of the cottages was owned by Salter's Brewery and was later converted into the presbytery behind the Catholic church.

133 Scotsbridge Mill was a fulling mill between 1692 and 1755, becoming a paper mill in 1757. A later owner was sued by the parish vestry for not paying his rates on the property. The mill closed down in 1881 due to chlorine entering the river Chess.

34 At the bottom of Scots Hill, Scotsbridge, 1912. On the left of the hill is Scotsbridge House, owned by Vice-Admiral the Hon. Josceline Percy between 1827 and 1856. Since 1953 it has housed the offices of the British Friesian Cattle Society. The entrance to Highfield House is on the right and the hill became part of the dual carriageway in 1972.

135 The Gospel Hall, Scots Hill, Croxley, pre-1940. A parachute bomb wrecked the hall in 1944, the blast damaging 210 houses in the immediate vicinity. The hall was relocated in Fuller Way.

136 At the top of Scots Hill, Croxley, 1903. The *George and Dragon*, a Salter's pub, is on the left of the picture with the shops clustered towards the top of the hill. Berean Cottages and the horse trough face the roadway and the Gospel Hall is to the right of the lamp-post.

37 Croxley windmill, Scots Hill, 1920. Constructed in 1820 as a brick tower carrying a cap with sails and fantail, lost its sails in a gale in the 1880s. It became dependent on steam power for its workings. During the Second World War, the windmill became a warden post and carried an air raid siren. It became a private house after the war.

38 All Saints' Church and Berean Cottages, Croxley Green. The church was enlarged and consecrated in 1908 as the population had grown, due partly to the expansion in the number of mill workers. The church was damaged by a parachute mine in 1940. Berean Cottages became known as Heroes Terrace when they were let to the soldiers of the First World War.

139 Providence Hall, The Green, Croxley Green, 1962. The house dates from *c*.1500 and is constructed of lathe and plaster. There is a baker's oven by the main fireplace.

140 *The Artichoke* public house, The Green, Croxley Green, 1910. The pub was owned in 1838 by Thomas Clutterbuck, a brewer of Stanmore, and it was a meeting place for the local Good Fellowship Society. It was also used for meetings with the solicitors over compensation for the loss of rights of common on Common Moor caused by the construction of the Watford to Rickmansworth railway.

141 Croxley House and the meeting of the Old Berkeley Hunt, The Green, Croxley Green. In 1767, the site of the present Croxley House was sold to Thomas, Lord Hyde, who became the Earl of Clarendon. He built the basis of the present house, and called it Grove Place. The Women's Voluntary Service bought the house in 1949 as a residential home for elderly people.

142 A procession of the Croxley Revels, 1964. The revels started in 1952, a queen with two attendants being chosen from the local primary schools. Here, Gibson's coal lorry is conveying the float carrying pupils of Harvey Road School in the procession. The coal firm closed in 1979.

143 Pre-fabs in Grove Crescent, Croxley Green, 1950. Built in 1946-7 by Rickmansworth council, just off Baldwins Lane, each of the small lanes had an individual name of a tree or shrub, except for Great Julians which was the name of the field on which they stood. Council houses now occupy the site along with Grove Crescent retirement flats which were opened in 1973.

144 Croxley Green Laundry Ltd., New Road, was situated opposite the corner of Yorke Road but later moved to Parkside, opposite Fortune Common at the bottom of Scots Hill.

145 The Dickinson Institute, Croxley Green. Founded by Mr. Charles Barton Smith, manager of Croxley Mill, the first institute opened in December 1895 combining a social club and reading room at 32 Milestone Field, later Dickinson Square. A larger building opened a year later with a concert and fireworks outside. In 1928 it became known as the House of Dickinson but burnt down in 1966.

146 New Road, Croxley Green, 1908. The Co-op was founded in Croxley Mills in 1887. It was registered a year later as the Croxley Co-operative Society, moving into two cottages in Dickinson Square. Later on, the premises moved to New Road where they are today. Robert Lindsay was the first manager of the society shop.

147 Gibbs the Blacksmith, New Road, Croxley Green. Jesse Gibbs started the business *c.*1899, in a smithy adjoining his house. His sons followed him in this trade and they also made cartwheels. His wife ran wagonettes to Watford market, price 6d. per head. The business lasted until the 1950s when the premises became Mead Autos.

148 The exterior of the Tithe Barn, Croxley Hall Farm. The barn was built in the 1400s when the manor of Croxley was producing large quantities of grain for St Alban's Abbey. The timber structural frame rises some 35ft. from flint foundation walls and is over 100ft. in length and 40ft. wide. It was roofed with handmade clay tiles.

149 The interior of the Tithe Barn, Croxley Hall Farm. There is a clear passage through this medieval barn from the doors either side to admit a fully laden hay cart and there are five stone walled bays on either side. Hertfordshire County Council bought the barn from Gonville and Caius College, Cambridge, in 1973 and gained an architectural heritage award for its restoration.

150 Cassio Bridge Wharf, *c*.1907—a temporary hold up of canal traffic. This view is towards Cassio Bridge Lock prior to the building of the railway viaduct. The bricks on the wharf could well be for building houses in the expanding town of Watford.

151 Unloading timber at Cassio Bridge Wharf, 1924. The view is from the viaduct carrying the Watford branch of the Metropolitan Railway and shows the wharf of Victoria Veneers, later Dareve's Moulding Mills. The timber was for the adjacent saw mill and the site is now a marina.

152 Croxley Mill, Common Moor. John Dickinson required a private Act of Parliament to build his paper mill on common land, purchased from Gonville and Caius College, Cambridge which held the rights of the lord of the manor of Croxley. The mill started production in 1830, the river Gade providing water power in the early days.

153 Delivering the goods to Croxley Mill. The materials to make paper were brought in by boat, as was coal once steam power was introduced. The narrow boats that took away the finished product were called paper dashers as they ran non-stop to London.

Rickmansworth to Batchworth Heath

54 Footbridge across the river Colne from Ebury Pleasure Grounds to Batchworth Lake, 1921. The landscaped gardens beside Batchworth Lake were laid out by Walker Bros., which also provided the former canal bridge (from West Herts. Golf Club) to link the lake with the gardens. These were officially opened by Lord Ebury in 1911 when Lady Ebury planted a commemorative tree.

155 *Below*. Batchworth Lake, *c*.1914. Walker's purchased the freehold of Batchworth Lake in 1913 for £3,800 from the Moor Park Estate. Access to the canal from the lake was opposite their boatyard. They provided a substantial boathouse, rowing boats, punts, and staging, and held their one and only regatta on the bank holiday of 3 August 1914—the day war was declared.

156 *Right*. Bury Lake in the 1930s. A syndicate called The Aquadrome Company acquired Batchworth Lake in 1928 together with Bury Lake, also a former gravel pit. They constructed a boathouse and moorings for sailing dinghies at the western end of Bury Lake and a commodious restaurant and clubhouse with an enclosure for swimmers together with a diving board.

157 *Below right*. The paddling area of Bury Lake. The Camping Club of Great Britain established a camp site on the northern side of the lake, towards Moneyhill. In 1939 the land was commandeered by the War Department for army exercises, and in 1960 it was bought by Rickmansworth council for £24,600.

THE AQUADROME, RICKMANSWORTH
L 1981

158 *Above left.* Stockers House, Grand Union Canal, was built adjacent to the lock by the Corporation of London for their collector of coal tax. It was built for £850 on land provided by Lord Ebury. Charles Browton was the first and only collector to live here, the office being abolished shortly afterwards. The house is now private.

159 *Above.* Frogmoor House, Harefield Road, 1964. The house was once owned by Emmot Skidmore, the last Quaker to be buried in the Quaker burial ground at Chorley Wood. The gardens were developed for housing in the 1950s and Frogmoor House was demolished in 1966 by Rickmansworth council. Flats built on the site for the elderly were opened in 1969 by Lord Balniel.

160 *Left.* The *White Bear* public house on the corner of Harefield Road, Batchworth, pre-1914, could date from the 1500s. It was mentioned in 1720 as *The Bear* and sometimes as the *Old Bear* and was owned by Salter's Brewery in 1838.

161 *Right*. The *White Bear* public house, Batchworth, 1914. A strip of land was purchased by Rickmansworth council to provide a pavement when the *White Bear* was rebuilt in 1914. The scene has hardly changed at all.

162 *Below*. Batchworth Bridge and Batchworth Island. To the left of the bridge are the stables which burned down in the 1950s. To the right is the island formed by the construction of the canal, and Batchworth Wharf on which Colin Taylor had his grinding mill, powered by steam rather than water.

163 *Below.* Batchworth Locks, Grand Junction Canal, 1907. The approach steps to the main lock were redesigned in this symmetrical form in 1899. Salter's Brewery constructed the left-hand lock in 1805 to give access to their brewery at Town Wharf. The house and stables on the right of the picture were originally owned by Matthew Pickford of Pickford Canal Carriers.

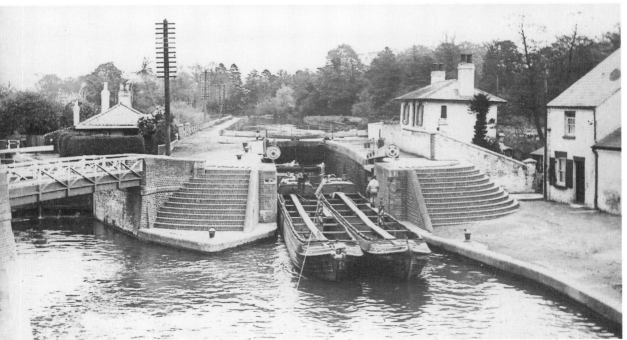

164 The *Railway Tavern* and *The Boat* public houses in Batchworth. The *Railway Tavern* was at street level and served railway travellers, while *The Boat* was at canal level serving boat people. The latter lost its licence in the 1920s and both buildings are now offices. In the days of horse drawn working boats there were stables here and on the other side of the bridge.

165 Batchworth Mill and hamlet, 1900. John Dickinson made paper in this mill in the early 19th century. It was later converted to a silk spinning factory and in 1900 the Rickmansworth and Uxbridge Valley Water Co. built a pumping station on the site. The 17th-century Batchworth House became a dower house for Lord Ebury's widow.

166 *Above.* The *Coach and Horses*, Batchworth. Tolls on the Harrow and Pinner turnpike were payable at this public house and a

167 Batchworth Charter Fair, 1960. The magical date of 17 May brought the annual delights of swingboats, hooplas, coconut shies, and other attractions to the small hamlet of Batchworth. In later years, only a handful of stalls and sideshows came to claim their ancient right to hold a fair.

169 Moor Park Old House. The house was built in 1663 by Sir Richard Franklin on farmland belonging to the Manor of the More. A later occupant was Mrs. Williams who lived here after her husband's death in 1814. The house was later demolished.

170 Moor Park Mansion, the home of Lord Anson (1730-63). The original mansion was built *c*.1675 for James, Duke of Monmouth. Benjamin Styles purchased the mansion in 1720 and clad the existing brickwork with Portland stone in the fashionable Palladian style at an alleged cost of £150,000. Admiral Lord Anson, the next owner, paid £80,000 for the house and employed Capability Brown to landscape the grounds.

171 Moor Park Mansion, 1903. A later owner, Thomas Bates Rous (1785-99) destroyed much of Styles' work by pulling down the colonnades and wings which housed the stables and servants' quarters. He rebuilt the kitchens beneath the house. During the ownership of the Marquess of Westminster, King William IV and Queen Adelaide were guests here at a magnificent garden party.

172 The painted ceiling of the entrance hall to Moor Park Mansion. The completely flat ceiling is painted to look like the dome of St Peter's in Rome. This lifelike painting was executed by Sir James Thornhill, a fashionable painter and architect, between the summer of 1725 and autumn of 1727. The great circle measures 20ft. in diameter.

173 Batchworth Heath, 1903. The heath was common land within the Manor of Batchworth and the gates in the background lead to Moor Park Mansion. *Ye Olde Green Manne* public house, a listed building of 16th- or early 17th century origin, was purchased by Salter's Brewery in 1838.

174 The first outing of the Rickmansworth Historical Society, outside St Mary's Church, July 1954. The society had just completed a tour of the historical sites of Rickmansworth under the leadership of Godfrey Cornwall. He was the inspiration of the society and chairman from its formation in May 1954 until his death in 1983.

Index

Roman numerals refer to pages in the introduction and arabic numerals to inividual illustrations

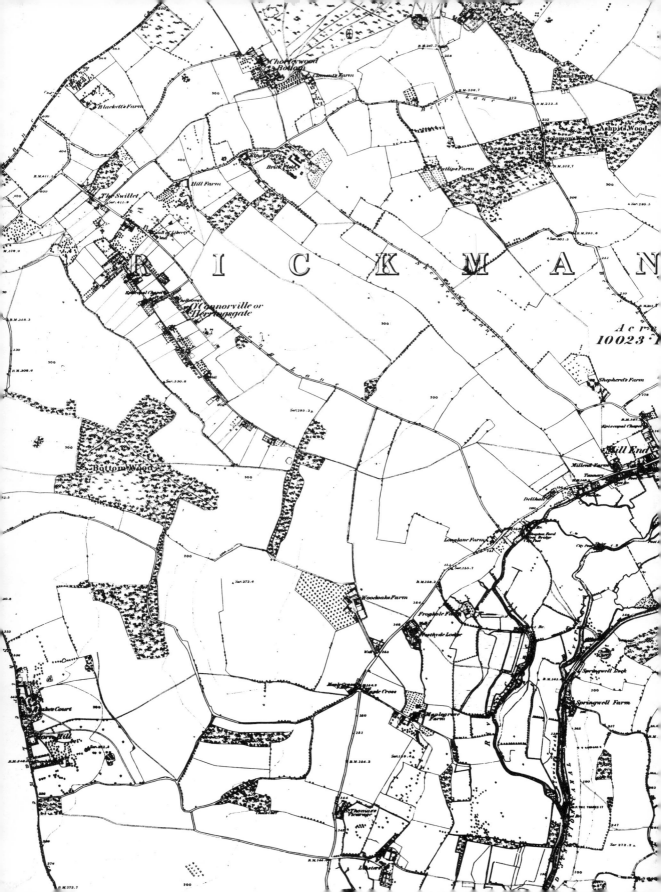